Prospecting

Increase Your Income and Learn How to Always Have a Full Pipeline of People Wanting to Buy from You Using Cold Calling, Social Selling, and Email

Volume 2

By

Income Mastery

Table of Contents

Introduction...5

Chapter 1: Take Advantage of Your CRM............6

Chapter 2: The Law of Familiarity 10

Chapter 3: Social Selling 13

Chapter 4: Our Message Matters..........................28

Chapter 5: Telephone Prospecting 32

Chapter 6: Learning to Manage RBOs: Reflex Response, When Customers Want to Get Rid of You, and Objections 35

Chapter 7: Who are Gatekeepers? 39

Conclusion 44

Glossary...46

Citation (APA Style)...51

Introduction

Do you want to be successful in business? Do you know how to do it? Do you know how to use the information you have? In the following book we will explain you how to use your CRM, that is to say, the Customer Relationship Manager program to be able to establish better relations with your contacts, to be able to create better proposals and with greater value to be able to sell your product and/or service. You'll also learn how to position yourself and your company so that people know you and trust your product more. Learn how to be successful, how to sell your product, how to get people in the industry to know you, to recommend you, but most importantly, learn how to build valuable relationships with your potential customers and how to turn a no into a yes.

Chapter 1: Take Advantage of Your CRM

In order to take advantage of CRM, Sales and Marketing must be aligned. Why? Because in order to take full advantage of CRM we must know who our target is and how we are going to sell our product and/or service. Let's start by explaining what "CRM" (Customer Relationship Manager) means. "Customer Relationship Manager" is a program to build Customer Loyalty. This program helps us improve relationships with our customers, find new prospects and regain lost accounts. How does this type of software work? This helps us to obtain and store valuable information from our customers. This will help us offer better products, personalize our emails and show you that we care about you as a customer. Also, as we have information about our clients, we can know or intuit what they need, which makes it easier for us to achieve a higher sale or sell you another product that will also be useful for your company.

This program will improve our interactions with customers. It is very important to keep track of every interaction we have with them. Again, this shows that we care about customers, we will have more information about them, and we can build better relationships, so we can continue to do business with them. When we take care of our prospects and customers, they will want to keep doing business with us. This type of software is very important and can be really useful or it can be a waste of money. Why? If your team doesn't understand the importance of storing each customer's information during each interaction and doesn't know how to use this information to sell better products and more efficiently in order to be more successful in sales, then the software doesn't work. This is the reason why it is really important that our team is trained as well as us to be able to make better decisions to achieve success.

You have to remember and give importance to the information you deserve. A small conversation with a client, no matter how short it is, will give us different ideas of what they are looking for, what their interests are, what their personality is, if we could sell them something more, what they need, among others. The entire team must be aligned and must understand this in order to be successful. On the other hand, remember that CRM lets you enter a lot of information. What is a way to build customer loyalty using this software? Congratulating you on your birthday. Just like that? Yeah, it's that simple. Why? Because everybody likes to be greeted on their birthday, if you don't want to or you don't have a budget, all you have to do is call them,that doesn't cost much. This will also give you a window so you can schedule a meeting with them if you do it in a professional and subtle way. Potential customers are going to be more open to listen to you if you're calling them not only to sell, but you're calling them to stablish a good relationship, in other words, yoe make them feel important for you. We can also send them an email with a birthday card or even just an email.

Why is this important? We must have a good relationship with our contacts, they must trust us, and they must feel that they are important to us. For example, if it's an important prospect, you can visit them with a present, like bringing them a small cake or some detail, this will also increase and give you a better relationship with them. Your prospects will feel that they have a relationship with you and that you are taking care of them and you care not only about their business but also about them as people. This is why it is so important to have this type of information in the CRM. Since we are recording all interactions with prospects or potential customers, we can also review this history and go visit them for their birthdays and give them presents. We must consider the CRM information, but we must sell it subtly, we cannot go just to sell because it is going to be a waste of time, money and energy. In order to form a friendlier and more trusting relationship, we can even take small notes such as when they mention if they are married, if they have children, what they like to do, what bothers them. This helps us to be able to ask a little more personal questions and let the prospects know that we are paying attention to them.

If we have a budget to invest in contacts and meetings, the CRM is very important because we can also add how much you have spent on our products, if you have asked for something additional, for example, or we can also add information on when you stopped working with us. We can segment this database into potential customers, and it can even help us recover customers. We can review what we had offered the client before and why he left, why he stopped working with the company. Having this information, we can call them with a better proposal, already knowing what is the problem they had. Remember that it is necessary that you investigate and have alerts and search for "trigger events" in order to have the window to recover a client or get more prospects and can become customers.

This customer database is also used to update it. Many times, the prospects move from their company and do not warn us, we can search in LinkedIn and update the data of both companies. We update the company and the name of the prospect who moved from the company, we look for who is the prospect in the previous company, and we can even look for who was the prospect in the person's new job from our database, this will not only make us update the database, but gain more prospects. Remember that when a prospect moves from their company, if he has a good impression of your company and you've made it look good in your previous job, he's going to want you to work with him in the new company. On the other hand, if the contact that has moved didn't want to work with you, now you have the window to work with a new person and the opportunity to sell him your business and turn him into a client.

Chapter 2: The Law of Familiarity

Do you know what the law of familiarity is? If prospects know your brand, have seen it on social networks or have heard from some people about it, they are much more likely to schedule a meeting with you, go to your events and trust your product and therefore you more. This will help generate and build your reputation in digital media and industry. It is very important to have positive comments which should be appreciated in order to generate interaction with customers and see that we care. On the other hand, if we have negative comments, it is very important to address them and show that we really care about our clients' feedback and that we will solve any mishap and adapt to the market and its needs.

Our prospects will look for us in social networks and they will see what comments we have to see who we have worked with and how our work with them has been. The law of familiarity indicates that our prospects had already heard of our brand, it is very important to consult how they have heard of us in different ways, they may have recommended us, that in these circumstances is optimal because they are people who have already worked with you and do not earn any commission or anything for recommending you for this is so important to have a good relationship with your customers and they will help you with recommendations.

It is really important to be constantly repeating the name of our company, always have it present, in emails, that it is on our business cards, that it is legible, always mention it at events, share articles from our website, get interviews in different media such as newspapers and articles from websites or social networks industry. All this will encourage more people to see the name of our company and at least remember the name when it is mentioned. In social networks, we can carry out different branding campaigns, that is, so that people know and see our brand there. We recommend that campaigns have a brief description of what the company does so that the audience that the ad is reaching can see the name and in front of the type of company and the industry in which it is in. Above all, it is important that people related to the company, always sell ourselves and our company as professionally as we can, remember that we are the face of our company.

How are you using your customers' data? Are you personalizing your emails? Are you using your customers' information to close deals with them? Small changes will make you have a better relationship with them, change their perception of you, make them trust you more, and make them feel "cockier" about you. This is going to be that they prefer to work with you even if your product is a little more expensive because you greet them for their birthday, you could send them something small like a cake, for example. These details are going to make you "win" the prospects. Worrying about them on a more personal level means that they not only trust us more, but also see that they are not just one more number for the company, but that we really care about them.

Now that you know how to identify a prospect and how to look for prospects. You will be able to make better decisions and spend less time and energy and get better results in our sales. This will lead to success. Remember not to be afraid to make calls to those prospects that are so necessary, check your competence, check how you are talking on the phone and it is really important that you know what your message is, that you know how to transmit it and that you always check with a colleague, colleague, or someone not within your organization if the message you are transmitting as well as the information is clear to the client. The practice makes the teacher! the more you practice, the better you will turn! Remember that you must maintain a good attitude and you must take care and pay attention to your habits. What do we mean by this? Stop procrastinating! Begin to carry out your work in the hours you have organized, do everything you have planned for the day. Look for prospects twenty-four hours a day, pay attention to your thoughts, change your thoughts and follow your day in a positive way. These small changes will make you have more sales, leading to success. If you're not achieving your purpose, don't be discouraged! Keep working hard. Remember that success never comes first, that we must work hard, change our habits, pay attention to what we are doing. Stay motivated and enjoy success!

Chapter 3: Social Selling

The Social Selling is in fashion, the objective is not directly the sale, but to make known our product, the attributes of the same one, to attract potential clients, to persuade and to converse with them. In other words, what we want is to begin the process of trust between the user and the brand. How do we do this? Social Selling is a sales model in which we use different social media, giving priority to LinkedIn. What we are implementing is a form of customer attraction based on branding, human relationships and developing useful content for our potential customers. This type of branding has appeared in recent years as we have all begun to use social networks. Now it is much easier to look for someone from a company and look for the position of the person we need to contact who would be interested in buying our products and who has a budget. All we have to do is send him a message. It's very important not to be intrusive, what do we mean by that? That we send messages correctly, present ourselves with names and surnames and send private messages.

Share useful content on your social networks, LinkedIn, Facebook and Instagram if you use it. Monitor how many visits you have, if you have interaction, what your prospects are interested in, how many views you have, among others. Remember that you must have a strategy and you must be constant in your social networks. What images are you using? Remember, even if you don't understand why it's so important that your photo is in high resolution, it's really important for customers to see your professional website because it could disqualify you as a provider if they don't like your website. Keep in mind that although Social Selling serves to maximize sales, it doesn't necessarily mean you're going to have an increase in sales. You are making your brand known, but it is necessary to analyze what the result is and whether the work is being done correctly in conjunction with Sales.

Let's start by thinking about who your target audience is and what social networks they are on. Don't forget to check the demographics and see where most users are because this is going to change by country or region. Usually the biggest B2B (business to business) is LinkedIn and Facebook because they have the largest number of users. Instagram is also important, and we can add it, but this will depend on our target audience, that is, who we want to sell to. Usually Instagram has a younger audience but still needs to be on this social network. LinkedIn and Facebook are slightly larger and wider audiences. How much we want and have to invest in each social network will depend on the product and the audience. The usual is to use all three platforms.

How to sell through social networks? Can it be measured? Of course, we do, first we have to decide what kind of campaign we want to do. What do we want? That more people know about us? Or sell a particular product and let people know about it. For example, if what we want is to generate awareness of our brand, that is, that people know us, we can invest in LinkedIn, which is the professional network where the majority of prospects are. This way, they'll see us. On the other hand, investing in Facebook Ads and Instagram ads, (you can manage Facebook and Instagram ads only from Facebook), where prospects may also be, but we will find gatekeepers and influencers as well.

The influencers are usually in charge of promoting the different products by talking about them and presenting them to their public, so they must be our target for them to see our advertisements. We must make interactive ads, for example, for Facebook is recommended to have as little text as possible, moreover, Facebook only lets the ads have twenty percent text, if it has more, the reach to the total number of people will be smaller. The more interactive and better the ad, the more people will want to enter our site. We must define and have an attractive advertisement, it can be a video, but it must be short, it can be a photo of our company or our product with a brief description and the link of our page.

We must remember that we can and must segment ads to reach the right people and make better use of the budget. Why do we recommend this? For example, if we are selling a specific product, we will have a specific market with certain characteristics and Facebook has the tool for us to segment and for advertising to be shown specifically to these people. We can place how much they should earn per year approximately, what type of position they should have and the type of education. This makes us go directly to the public, who are our potential customers and who could become our customers. We have to decide how long we are going to carry out this campaign and how much we are going to invest. It is very important to be able to monitor the ad all the time and see if we are getting the desired result. Not only do we need to verify how many people our ad is reaching, if they are entering our website, if they are clicking on the ad or if they are sharing or asking for more information. It is also important to talk with sales and see if they are calling them directly, if they have more prospects, if they are scheduling more visits, among others.

It happens many times that people see your ad in some social network, and instead of writing to you by   they call directly to the number that appears in the ad. It is really important that the ads have our company's phone number written correctly, an email to write to, an address and it is relevant and even the website. In this way we can see how many people are being redirected and we can see the conversion and whether our ad is well done. If we are not receiving calls, are not writing, do not enter our website and we are not having a positive response, we need to pause the ad and focus on seeing what happened and deal with a new ad. Many times, we think something is going to work and it doesn't, we just have to start over and see if the new strategy works. This may not have worked because the art was not well designed, suddenly Facebook accepted it for advertising (pattern) but as it has so much text is not being shown to the amount of people that could come or suddenly, we have segmented in the wrong way. Suddenly we have made a mistake, we can change the segmentation and start again until we get to the right segmentation and start having positive responses from our potential customers.

At the end of each campaign, we must make a table with the amount of money we have invested for each social network, how much has been the value per click in the ad, how much reach we have achieved, how many impressions we have achieved, how many times the ad has been shared, or have made comments. It is very important that if you write to your inbox, i.e. by private message, you reply in a professional manner, quickly and send the necessary information.

If we can collect data, it would be better to enter it into the CRM. With the name of the person who appears in the profile, we can do a quick search on LinkedIn and see if it could be a prospect, it is worth noting, that many times the competition also writes and they will write to us because they are doing market research. What do we mean by this? They are analyzing their competitors. What is their price, what is what they are offering, how do they offer it, what is their proposal, how do they respond, what kind of promotions do they have, among others. We need to take this into account and do some research.

We must also do market research. Before launching a campaign, we must investigate the competition as well. How do I know who my competition is? Basically, they are companies similar to yours, which have similar products within the same region. What does it mean that they are in the same region? It means the potential customers will be the same as yours. This type of competition is called direct competition because the value of the product and what is offered to the prospect is very similar. Suddenly we want to do a kind of campaign to build customer loyalty, but we must be careful not to reveal too much in social networks. We must analyze the campaigns before carrying them out, suddenly a loyalty campaign is better carried out by mail with a good database. Note that databases can also buy it. If you really don't know where to start, suddenly buying a good segmented database can be a good place to start. You can also run campaigns on social networks to increase your database in which they ask prospects, or, the people to whom the ad is being shown to leave you their personal data. Of course these people won't give it to you if you're not giving them something in return, unexpectedly it's a ten percent discount on their next purchase, suddenly you want them as subscribers to your blog or suddenly you're going to hold a draw giving them one of your products or you can ally with a company in a contest for people to follow your page, the other person's and give themselves a product. In case you want to have subscribers on your company's blog, remember that the content you share must be of good quality and useful to potential customers. The more interesting it is and if they can really put this information to good use, the more followers you will get in less time.

We must always take care in social networks spelling and that the photos we upload are of good quality, so they do not look like "pixelated". The client will know that we care and that we are not neglected if we have a good website. It perceives us as a more serious company, with more knowledge, that cares about making a good impression and that everything is fine. In order to start advertising on social networks, it is important to have an annual schedule. We recommend that this be worked on the previous year and that you work in conjunction with sales. We must consider special dates such as Black Friday, Halloween, holidays of the country where your company is and the holidays or important days according to the different industries. Why are we talking about important days for industries? In case we want to sell a software to a tourism company, we can use that day to send an email to our contacts who should be entered in our CRM greeting and congratulating them on the day of tourism. Of course, it looks like a harmless mailing, but this makes people know you and is more likely to open your mail. , They must have your data, your website and what it does to the company so that they can enter to review.

What is outbound marketing? Have you heard of it? Outbound marketing is a direct sales channel to a specific audience, call it our "target market". How do we do this? Let's start by generating a list of all the companies and prospects in those companies that we think are good prospects and could buy our product. Once this is done, we must call them and during this call find out if they are indeed people who would be interested in buying our products, that is, if they are prospects. This is for B2B companies. This list, which can be generated by us, by sales with marketing or by software, is a list of prospects or leads that could become our customers. This also includes sending an email before calling the customer. It is also important that we take into account and know what the content of our website is, this way, it is easier to direct prospects to the page so that we can show you the product that suits your needs.

Events, the content of our website, social networks, discussion forums and / or newsletters may improve communication with our client and help him understand more about our product and us will help us better explain our product. It is very important that all our communication is clear and concise, and that we don't offer more than we can fulfill because we could be catalogued as misleading advertising and that the photographic material, if we are using that is usually the case, is clear and true. Videos help customers better understand how the product works, what the product's advantages are, and exactly what our product does. It is very important to have a short version of the product apart from a longer demonstration video as we are trying to increase our interaction and increase the possibility of our prospects becoming our customers.

Do you think that social selling is everything and that it will lead to success? No, we always find problems with social sales. When using social networks, we must be very clear about what we are promoting, how we are promoting it, who our target audience is, what we want to achieve with this promotion and we must consider the language we are using.

Why is this important? Let's say we know the law of familiarity and we want more people to know our company. Let's just say we're using social networks, in this specific case Facebook. We decided that we want to pay Facebook, so that more people know our company. Let's start with how much budget we're going to invest and for how long. Here we must know that the budget and time in which we have the promotion will vary the number of people we reach. Now, let's begin. What's the purpose of our campaign? We want more people to know us and follow us on social networks. Perfect, now, who is the segment I should be targeting? How can I segment the audience in social networks? We have the option to choose and segment the people who can see our advertising. For example, let's start with the basics, where is our company located? We want to advertise locally, nationally or internationally. After we have decided this, we can choose the interests of the people we are going to advertise to. What is the socioeconomic level of people who are within our segmentation? Are they people with what kind of studies? Do they have any particular interests? Do they share a particular characteristic? By analyzing this, we can realize if it is better, that we recommend it, to advertise directly to our target audience or if we choose the default option of the pattern which is advertising with a radius of at least twenty-five kilometers.

Now, after campaigns it's always good to check our metrics, also known as KPIs. We must see if our efforts have gone to the right people and if we have made good use of our budget, if we have had queries about our company, if we have received more calls, if we have arranged more meetings with our prospects, if our list of prospects has grown, among others. It is very important to do an analysis after campaigns. Sales must work together with marketing so that sales can tell you what you need to achieve.

Now, another very important point is personal branding, do you know what we mean by that? We must do our own marketing. How? Should we also do personal marketing? Yes, of course I do. We can achieve this by going to events, known as networking events, or events where we know we will be able to meet and possibly discover our prospects. It is important to go, not hide behind people and present ourselves to prospects with our full name. We recommend not giving out our card before introducing ourselves and squeezing the hands of the prospects, this way, they will have a better impression of you, they will be able to establish a better relationship with you and they will not think that the only thing you want from them is their money.

Also, our social networks and LinkedIn say a lot about us. Let's take a minute to review our social networks, how is our name written? Is it easy to find each other? What profile picture do we have? Is it professional? We must remember that social networks and our photos there, what we share, publish, write, comment, appear and our prospects can also investigate us. Prospects get an idea of who we are and what kind of service or even how good our information-based product is on our social networks.

Now, do you have pictures taken? incriminating pictures, pictures at many parties, drunken pictures? Take them back now! We want to give our prospects the impression that we are serious, hard-working people, that we are responsible and that the value of our brand is commensurate with our actions. Why do we emphasize this? Because we represent the brand, the way we behave reflects our brand and vice versa. What are you waiting for to check your social networks! Pay attention to which groups you are following, what you are commenting on and what your language is like.

Now, let's continue with LinkedIn. We must have one, even if we don't like social networks, we don't know or understand very well how it works, it is very important and urgent to have a good profile on LinkedIn. We must place all our relevant information, which presents us as experienced professionals. Fill out information about your studies, some additional courses, certifications you have taken, the languages you speak, and it is also important that you fill in your skills. Now, LinkedIn is letting us fill mini exams that certify that we know how to use or have the skills we say we have, for example in Microsoft Excel. They are exams that last between five and ten minutes and LinkedIn give us the certificate which is good because it is no longer a partner or someone who knows you, it is an objective test performed on a computer.

Let's continue with inbound marketing, inbound marketing is to generate leads by creating different attractive content for potential customers and asking prospects for information such as their name, email and phone number, in order to prepare some information that will be useful for them. This generates leads. Now, are all these people valuable and should we consider them as prospects? Should we focus only on them? No, there are people who want to download our content that are really valuable, but there are others who are just leaving their data because the information is valuable for a job at the university or because they need it for any other reason. Now, yes, we have to assume that each person who downloads our information is a lead and works until he has the information he is looking for. For example, if we have a subscriber who has only left us his name and email, we should investigate him and treat him as a lead. How do we do this? Let's look for it on LinkedIn, let's try to gather all the information we can to see who this person is, where he works and if he could be a prospect. Equally, it is important, as we have already mentioned, to have the information and to keep the interactions with the customers. We don't know when we might need it, suddenly, the person writes us from his email, and we can see what content he downloads. This will help us to put together a more personalized proposal and we already know what your interests are.

Now, let's continue with the trigger events and the purchase cycle. Activation events are interruptions in the status quo that opens purchase windows and can force buyers to take different measures. What do we mean by this? We can follow our prospects on social networks without being directly connected to them. For this reason, we must be constantly monitoring its flow of news, lists, update alerts, discussions in groups, among others to be aware and take advantage of the "trigger events. This means that we will be able to contact prospects at the right time so that we can introduce ourselves and our project to them when they really need it. As we have already mentioned, if you are asking for a company that has similar characteristics to ours, if you ask for the data of different companies, if you comment in a group, among others, will be our window to offer you our services.

Now, why is it so important to research and gather information? Because on social networks there is too much information from prospects, so they don't notice. This will help us enter our database, we can develop messages and prospecting campaigns based on your interests and we can plan the call, our message or our email. We can know beforehand what you need for your company, whether you have complained about a particular brand and what your interests are. This can also break the ice in the conversation and find something in common with the prospect. This can be the difference between a prospect becoming a customer and remaining a prospect.

On the other hand, outbound prospecting refers to the collection of data from potential customers. How do we achieve this? For example, universities or construction companies request certain information in their social media campaigns so that they send you the price list. They usually ask for an email address, name, contact number and even your ID number. People fill it in because the information is easier to get this way. This feeds our database and increases our number of prospects; they have already contacted us which means they are interested in our products. This is going to help us increase our prospects. As they leave us the telephone or the electronic mail, we can contact them, call them or send them an electronic mail. Again, we recommend that you look for the contact, investigate about him, what his interests are, among others. We can and recommend using social networks together with data collection to get better results, more leads, better prospects and increase our database. We recommend to carry out a campaign in social networks to generate familiarity with our company, so that people know our brand and know what we do and in parallel we can collect data with different types of promotions and / or advertise an article from our blog on our website for example to increase our subscribers.

It is very important to follow the personal data laws by country for the use of personal data. Usually, a clause has been added in the format where we are requesting the information. These efforts increase our chance of success and help us with prospecting.

Chapter 4: Our Message Matters

What are you going to say and how are you going to say it? This is really important as it helps us to improve communication with our customers. What do we want to convey to the customer? What is our message? We recommend writing down all the attributes of our product and/or service as we tend to forget some of the information and not provide it completely. This should be done before sending an email or calling a prospect so that we can provide the information and not forget some piece of information that may be key to turning a potential customer into a customer. What can we do to see if we are delivering the right message to the prospect? You can, for example, do a simple exercise, talk to a colleague or a friend and pretend a call. They will be the potential customer, that is, the prospect. Let's pretend we're calling them or we're sending them an email with the information we would send to a potential customer. You have to take this person and this exercise seriously and investigate it in order to send a correct email, and communicate with them by phone, that is, with a cold call. We need to call them and talk like we'd really do a potential customer. Now we must ask the following questions after the exercise Is the information, we are providing understood? Are we being clear? Do I sound very cold on the phone? Do you understand what my product is about and how it can benefit you? Do you think I am cold or professional on the phone? What do you think of my tone of voice? Do I sound false or do I sound enthusiastic and reliable?

Many times, we think that we are giving information the right way, it is important to be open to constructive criticism. After having all the feedback of this interaction, we must continue practicing to improve. Remember that practice makes the master. Don't you know how to give the message? Find a mentor or pay attention to your colleagues, examine how they are giving the message over the phone, then you can figure out your own way to do it. On the other hand, we must always remember to be clear and concise with the information and take care of our tone. It is important that we understand that as we know the product, we can think that we are giving the customer all the information they need and our partner realizes that we are not.

Also, we can make small mistakes such as forgetting to introduce ourselves with our full name, the name of the company, we have spoken very quickly, we didn't give the name of the company well, we interrupted the client or didn't let him speak, among other fairly common mistakes that we usually make without realizing it. The problem with performing the same task daily or often, is that we usually automate and stop paying attention. This is why it is important that every one or two weeks, we revisit how we are communicating and if we need to make some adjustments. When we are giving our message, we must speak with enthusiasm and confidence. We must believe in what we are saying and be able to convey confidence to the customer that not only our product is good, but we also know the product, that we will be able to resolve their doubts and if they have a problem, we will be able to resolve it because we have all the information and the attitude and desire to want to help them.

It is very important that we know what the added value of our product is, what is the customer going to gain by hiring me? 24-hour remote technical support? What can I offer you that the competition cannot offer you? This point is very important because the client will choose us if he feels at ease with us, if he feels that he has our support and feels that he is going to obtain a benefit greater than the cost. It's very important to know what we want. We have to start with this. On the other hand, speaking of the message, the way we behave when we go to meetings is very important. How did we sit at the table? Did we let the customer feel first? Am I with my arms folded? Am I leaning back? Am I looking at the cell phone? We recommend that you pay attention to the details which is where the difference between a prospect and a client lies. For example, if we are sitting back in the chair with our arms crossed, the contact is going to think that we don't want to be there, even worse, if we are with our legs stretched out. We can sit slightly with the body forward, this way the client realizes that we are listening, and our body language is positive. We must smile as we give our message, shake our head so that the client knows we are listening. Now, how are we giving our message during the presentation? Remember that we must conform to the companies we are going to visit, but that doesn't mean that we should just concentrate on this. We must subtly emphasize why our company is better than the others, why they should work with us and how your company will benefit from the use of our products or services.

Chapter 5: Telephone Prospecting

We must begin by making the call we fear so much to our prospects. If we already have our prospect's phone number, we should start preparing to call them. We must have a list of all our prospects in order of importance. We must always remember to investigate prospects and their company before calling them. We must ask ourselves and know what is it that they need for their company? We must remember what questions our prospect might ask, but at the same time, we must remember not to saturate with information. We must be concise and dare to make the call. What is the worst that can happen? Tell us that you are not interested? We must be attentive to the telephone, call them and introduce ourselves with our full name and the name of the company, we must tell them why we have called them and what we want. We must also remember to be modular and clear so that the potential customer can understand us correctly. We must speak slowly, slowly and with a good tone. These calls must be short, that is to say, we cannot pretend that we will give you all the information of the company by telephone, we will saturate them. Apart from that they are not going to understand what the company is for and what our product really is.

If this is your first time calling a prospect, we can corroborate your email address so we can send you more information. During telephone prospecting, we must also consider whether the potential customer we are actually talking to is a potential customer, or whether we have made a mistake.

Are you terrified of calling because you don't want to be hung up on the phone? Have you ever been hung up on the phone? What do you start screaming about on the phone? Have you ever called a prospective client and started telling you all their intimate stories because at that moment they were sad or needed to talk to someone? Listen to them and don't interrupt them. Sometimes prospects think we're friends and that confuses the relationship. We must always remain professional; everything must be handled with the confidentiality that the prospects deserve.

Is there a way to turn a rejection into a sale? We'll explain this in the next chapter. Did you see that? There's nothing to be afraid of. We cannot emphasize enough how important it is to do an investigation prior to the call, if we don't do it, the client will realize and won't think that we are professionals and won't trust us. This can be the difference between setting up a meeting and having your phone hung up or not being answered again. We have to be smart when it comes to making the call. Not only do you have to give information, you also have to ask the person what they need. For example, if we start talking about the daily challenge's companies face and how our product can help you, let's ask if you have any of the challenges mentioned above or if you have any other challenges. This will not only help us gather more information from the prospectus, we will also be able to feed our CRM and we will be able to personalize the proposal that we will present at the meeting. We will be able to further investigate this particular type of challenge which will cause a better impression on the prospect, which in turn will generate trust and a better relationship which will increase the opportunity to close the business. Let's not forget that we also have to see in every call whether the potential customers or prospects are really prospects. What do we mean by that? That many times we are sure that a prospect is until we talk to him. We can tell by your position, experience or by the type of response or questions the prospect asks us as well as the type of comments.

Chapter 6: Learning to Manage RBOs: Reflex Response, When Customers Want to Get Rid of You, and Objections

When we're working in our business, it's very easy to feel vulnerable. Do you know how to deal with rejections? Rejection is hard to handle if we don't know how to do it. Calling customers is usually the most stressful part of a salesperson's day. If you are rejected, it is very easy to feel unmotivated and even afraid to call customers. Let's get started, when you phone you can follow this simple five-step process: Call and get the attention of the prospect, identify yourself with your full name and tell the prospect where you are calling from, explain what it is you want and continue with why. This is crucial because you have to tell them what the benefit is and how it can help your prospect in his day-to-day life, but in a concise and objective way. Go ahead and tell them what you want, for example, if you want a meeting with them, if you'll be sending information to their email and then you want to meet with them.

When you're talking to a prospect, either on the phone or in person, you'll encounter three types of rejection. A reflex response from a prospect in this case could be "don't worry, we're fine". This kind of answers cut off the conversation and don't let you expand and sell your product. This type of rejection is quite common. When a customer wants to get rid of you, he doesn't want to talk to you, the well-known "brush-off" will probably tell you, why don't you just send me the information? In the category of customer rejections, we will also find real objections. For example, if a prospective customer has just signed with another company for a product similar to yours. It is very important to know how to deal with these responses on their part, as this does not indicate 100% rejection. We should know that we have a couple of options after receiving this type of response and that an objection by the prospect does not necessarily mean that we have failed, only that we can and should take some necessary action. The important thing is to know how to flip an objection and turn it into a sale.

Now, there are three alternatives to which we can turn. We must begin to design simple scripts that we can repeat without having to think and without letting our emotions influence, this is of utmost importance since we cannot change the tone of voice and we must not let the prospect realize that we have been affected by his response. This script must sound natural. For example, a typical response that sounds natural, but is a memorized and automatic response might be "I thought you could say that. This is going to help change the pattern of the conversation, the prospect probably won't expect such an answer and you can go on, we must say something really attractive that gives us a chance to win the prospect.

It also works to interrupt the prospect, I know it sounds strange, but this also breaks the pattern, the answer and if you choose well what you are going to mention next, you can attract the prospect to you. For example, a typical answer is "Perfect, if you get great prices and services, you shouldn't think about changing. All I want is a few minutes of your time to learn more about your company and see if we're fit. For example, if a prospect responds with a "I'm not interested," a model response would be, "yes, many people tell me that when I first call, but that's exactly why we should get together. We can't emphasize enough that it's important to learn our emotions and ask the prospect again, in a super positive way, but being assertive, what we want to get from that call, we can follow the answer script if this makes us nervous or difficult. As we work through these scripts, we must sound authentic, sure of what we are offering, but most importantly, we must not let our emotions cloud us. In this way we can not only deal with this setback, with this type of response, but we can also achieve a sale, even if we had an initial rejection by the prospect.

We also need to know when not to keep trying, to be resilient and to know how to turn an objection into a sale is one thing, but we need to know when a prospectus is not going to receive us, it is not really a prospectus and it is not going to want to meet us if we are on the phone. If we are in a face-to-face meeting, we must also know how to end a meeting if our prospect is not receptive, makes too many excuses and is not going to buy our product or contract our services. Let's not waste any more time and energy on this type of prospects, we must take them off our list and be awaiting a change of prospect in charge of that area in that company.

Chapter 7: Who are Gatekeepers?

What's a gatekeeper? What do we mean by that? It is usually a sales assistant or some executive assistant, a person within a corporation who can influence the purchase of a product. They work closely with the decision maker. If you're an assistant, chances are you know your boss's problems and have to deal with them, so getting your product will benefit them, too. It's very important to sell and communicate our products to them in the same way we would to their boss, why? These prospects not only influence the decisions, if it will also help them to have less workload, they could even recommend how to present our products and tell us a little bit about why it is necessary. Work with them as allies and you'll see how much the gatekeepers can help you by trying insights and different ways of presenting the product to the person who makes the decision to secure a sale of our product. Never fail to consider it.

Now, we have another type of person in the organization who can help us sell our product and have a successful meeting with the decision maker, these people usually have a junior level and compare the products and their characteristics to see what is most beneficial to the company. This person can be categorized under the name of influencer, so that they do not make the decision directly, just as their opinion has weight and can influence the sale. We must identify who this person is, have a meeting with them, explain in the best way, directly and concisely what is the benefit that the company earns and how it can benefit him and his collaborators to work with us. It is very important to meet with this person because they are going to help us and provide us with valuable information about the company's processes, they are going to explain the problems they face every day, what they are doing to avoid and/or fix them and how we can present our business to the person who decides to incline to work in our company.

On the other hand, when we meet with the person who makes the decision and has the budget, we will already have this information and a clearer idea of how to sell our product because the influencer and the gatekeeper have already told us the problems they have to deal with every day. This information will help us enormously because we will go with more personalized and detailed information focused on the specific needs of the client. This will give more security to the prospect and help us build a better relationship with them from the beginning. The prospect will know that we have researched their needs and will realize that our product is exactly what they need. It is necessary to go to the meeting prepared and explain everything in a short and concise way, always emphasizing the benefit for them as a company, how they can improve their processes, their productivity and above all increase their income.

How do you recognize a person with the power to decide? These prospects usually hold senior positions, such as Manager, Director, Vice President and the

Managing Director. These prospects are what we should be looking for, we should concentrate on meeting with them, and if we cannot, it is important that we meet first with the influencer and if we can with the gatekeeper as well. They will recommend to the person making the decision to meet with us, as senior managers do not accept so many meetings and less with people who are not recommended.

Meeting with the influencer and gatekeeper, helps us to get in touch with the person who makes the decision, to go to the meeting more informed, to sell our product better and to pay more attention to us. Also meeting earlier with the influencer and gatekeeper, helps us make the decision maker more open to listening to us and to prepare and ask us the right questions to measure how this will benefit your company, that this person also researches the product before the meeting.

On the other hand, it also happens that we find neither the gatekeeper, nor when influencing and there is no way to communicate with the prospect, how to schedule meetings with them? Ask your sales colleagues and friends if anyone knows him or someone in that company and if it would be feasible for them to introduce you. Being recommended or introduced by a colleague is very important because it means that this person trusts you. The decision maker will also meet with you with a more open mind about your product. Now, it's important to keep in mind that there are "influencers" that are "toxic" and will waste our time. What do we mean by that? That this person will make comments such as "I can help you talk to the manager", "I can influence him", "my salary is x amount", or "the director and I are friends". This type of people usually make us loose time, the truth is that they have no influence, nor do they know the director or manager of the company. We must know how to recognize them and treat them as such.

So how do I recognize them? They are people who are going to give you too much information without you asking for it, they are going to tell you that they have a lot of authority in the company, that they have a lot of weight and a lot of responsibility. What questions to ask them? Ask them when and how they meet with managers. The executive assistants or influencers do have contact with them, they usually have weekly, biweekly or monthly meetings. If you're thinking of a particular person, congratulations, you've learned to differentiate them. When this happens, we should look for another contact in the company that can help us reach the prospect. We often confuse prospects with people who make recommendations to the prospect. It is also important to have this information and know how to recognize them, they are not prospects, but they are valuable for us because they can help us by recommending or giving us information about what is needed in the company before having the meeting with the prospect.

On the other hand, if we stop answering emails and calls, it is important that we make a decision, if the person was not the right one, if it is not really an influence for example and we should seek another contact, or if we should stop wasting time with that company. It is important before thinking that we are wasting time with a company that we are looking for in LinkedIn who are the people in charge, what position has the person with whom we were talking and if there is another way or another person who can help us get to the prospect in case we cannot call him directly. For these reasons we must learn to recognize them, we must learn how to communicate with them and learn to manage our emotions. We must be expressive and sound enthusiastic. If we trust ourselves, the customer will also trust us. Call them, get meetings with them, analyze and research their companies and you will see that when you meet with the gatekeeper or influence, you must have all the right information and have analyzed the company so that these potential customers can become your customers.

Conclusion

As you may have seen, there are different ways to reach our potential customers. We must look for what their interests are, what they need to improve their sales, their productivity, collect as much information as we can from them and your company to be able to present a proposal that they find attractive and interesting. Also, it is very important to know who to communicate with in the company that could facilitate the sale, there are different people like the gatekeeper for example or influencers who could help us and give us more information on how the sale works and could even give us recommendations on how to present our product to the person who is responsible for deciding. We must remember that we can always meet people we can consider "toxic" because they say they have influence or some kind of decision-making power in the purchase of your product and/or service when it is not true. We must learn to recognize them and stop wasting our energy and time on them. Also, we must also learn when it's time to let go of a prospect, not everyone will buy your product. We must also know when the right time is to offer our product. Remember that we have two volumes with strategies, techniques and recommendations for you to achieve success. It is advisable to study the principles of these books with great attention; it is highly recommended to opt for additional sources of information to complement the learning. Don't forget that all this has been done for you, the readers, with much passion and dedication for this subject. Prospecting is an art, and we can only learn from it if we take action. Let's not stay at the reading. Let's go for more.

Glossary

Prospectus: A potential client is a person or company with whom we have no business relationship but whose interests could make him a client. Today's prospect is tomorrow's customer.

Segmentation: Segmentation divides a market into smaller segments of buyers who have different needs, characteristics and behaviors that require differentiated marketing strategies or mixes. For example, we can segment our prospects, i.e. potential customers, prospects in the CRM, among others.

Emailing's: Sending emails to several emails simultaneously oriented specifically to sell. This allows us to retain, build loyalty, send promotions and important information to our customers. We can have several different mailing lists.

Cold calling: Make calls to potential customers.

CRM : Program that helps Customer Management in an organized way.

Gatekeeper: A person within a company or organization, usually a management executive or executive assistant. This person is valuable because he or she can influence the prospect's decision. In this case, we must know how to deal with it. They usually know what the organization's problems are and our product could also simplify their work.

Linkedin: It is a professional social network for companies and where normal people can put information about where we work, what has been our education, experience, skills and qualities. Additionally, we can certify with the new LinkedIn certificates. We can have LinkedIn on our Android and IOS operating systems or on the computer.

Networking

Facebook: Social network where we can communicate with different people in different parts of the world. It is a way to share content in a simple and fast way on the Internet. It is available for the Android and IOS operating systems.

Instagram: Instagram is a social network and application. Its function is to upload photos, videos. It's available for Android and iOS devices.

The Universal Law of Necessity: The Universal Law of Necessity dictates that the more you need to sell something, the less likely you are to sell it. I know it seems confusing, but let's get this example straight. Let's just say that Rodrigo hasn't searched or contacted many prospects during the month, now, he needs to close contacts, but he just stayed and has some opportunities.

Law of thirty days: Law of thirty days dictates that the prospects you have worked for thirty days will bear fruit in the following ninety days; this means that the more prospects you work in a month in a row, that is, the more you work in the year, the more fruits, call for example commissions you will get due to the increase in prospects.

Procrastination: This is when you do some other activity before starting your work, i.e., or priority.

Perfectionism: Perfectionists also tend to take too long or not use the work we've been doing so well; everything seems horrible to us. Additionally, we are going to take too long to perform a simple task, is this worth it?

Paralysis: it is real, and this happens when we have stopped doing some activity and it tells us to start again. For example, many writers stop writing and feel that they have failed, find it hard to start over because they feel that they are not good enough or that they cannot start, that they will never be as creative as the other person and that they do not have enough potential, that is, they feel as if they are losers.

Corollary of Hortsmans: Principles to be taken into account in order to achieve better sales, more productivity in the team and more success.

Social Selling: Social Selling is a sales model in which we use different social media, giving priority to LinkedIn. What we are implementing is a form of customer attraction based on branding, human relationships and developing useful content for our potential customers.

B2B: Business to business or company to company.

Gatekeeper: A person within a corporation who can influence the purchase of a product. They work closely with the decision maker. You could be an assistant and most likely you know your boss's problems and have to deal with them, so getting your product will benefit them too.

Influencer: Now, we have another type of person in the organization who can help us sell our product and have a successful meeting with the decision maker, these people usually have a Junior level and compare the products and their characteristics to see what is most beneficial to the company. This person can be categorized under the name of influencer, they do not make the decision directly, just as their opinion has weight and can influence the sale.

Toxic Influencer: People who impersonate an influence but are not. They will usually say that they have a good position in the company, that they have a good relationship with their superiors, that they earn a lot of money and that they have a lot of money. They're gonna give out a lot of information without us asking for it.

Trigger Event: It is an event that can generate sales. For example, a prospect changed company and this appears on LinkedIn. How does it impact our company? It could generate a window for a sale in the new company where you are working and could generate an additional sale in the old company.

Google Alerts: These are alerts that we can configure in Google so that we receive different news depending on what we configure. For example, each time there is a press release, an alert will be sent to the cell phone or device we have configured.

Citation (APA Style)

1. Beatriz Soto, B. S. (2018a, 17 October). What is mailing? Discover everything related to the sending of massive mails. Retrieved October 5, 2019, from https://www.gestion.org/que-es-el-mailing/
2. Carlo Farucci, C. F. (n.d.). How to calculate #ROI in #MarketingDigital? Retrieved October 5, 2019, from https://josefacchin.com/roi-retorno-de-inversion/
3. Definition of prospection - Definicion.de. (n.d.). Retrieved October 5, 2019, from https://definicion.de/prospeccion/
4. Douglas Burdett, D. B. (s.f.). Sales Prospecting Without Social Media Is Like Selling Without a Phone. Recuperado 5 octubre, 2019, de https://www.salesartillery.com/blog/sales-prospecting-social-media-selling
5. Fanatical Prospecting: The Ultimate Guide to Opening Sales Conversations and Filling the Pipeline by Leveraging Social Selling, Telephone, Email, Text, and Cold Calling. (s.f.). Recuperado 5 octubre, 2019, de https://www.oreilly.com/library/view/fanatical-prospecting-the/9781119144755/20_chapter12.html
6. Jesús L. Cortiñas, J. L. C. (2016, 27 April). Is the prospect...? - Management Notes. Retrieved

October 5, 2019, from https://www.apuntesgestion.com/b/la-prospeccion-es/

7. Jonathan Ebenstein, J. E. (2016, 28 abril). 5 tips for leveraging your CRM data. Recuperado 5 octubre, 2019, de https://www.bizjournals.com/bizjournals/how-to/marketing/2016/04/5-tips-for-leveraging-your-crm-data.html

8. Josh Slone, J. S. (2019, 27 septiembre). Cold Calling Techniques That Actually Work – Gist. Recuperado 5 octubre, 2019, de https://getgist.com/cold-calling-techniques-that-actually-work/

9. Krishna Srinivas, K. S. (2018, 23 octubre). 12 Techniques to Write a Sales Prospecting Email that Surely Gets Responses. Recuperado 5 octubre, 2019, de https://blog.klenty.com/prospecting-email-sales/

10. The 8 most useful prospecting methods for your company. (2019a, 9 July). Retrieved October 5, 2019, from https://clickbalance.com/blog/contabilidad-y-administracion/metodos-de-prospeccion/

11. The 8 most useful prospecting methods for your company. (2019b, July 9). Retrieved October 5, 2019, from https://clickbalance.com/blog/contabilidad-y-administracion/metodos-de-prospeccion/

12. MC Donald, D. E. V. O. N. (2010, 16 septiembre). Outbound Prospecting Defined | OpenView. Recuperado 5 octubre, 2019, de https://openviewpartners.com/blog/outbound -prospecting-defined/

13. Nicole Mertes, N. M. (2019, 6 septiembre). Traditional Prospecting vs. Inbound Prospecting. Recuperado 5 octubre, 2019, de https://www.weidert.com/whole_brain_market ing_blog/traditional-prospecting-vs.-inbound-prospecting

14. NIDKEL, A. N. (2017, 25 mayo). The Hub and Spoke Model for Marketing: The Wheel is Still King | CNP. Recuperado 5 octubre, 2019, de https://cnpagency.com/blog/the-hub-and-spoke-model-for-marketing-the-wheel-is-still-king/

15. Olga Milevska, O. M. (2019, 4 julio). What is Prospecting? Definition and Best Methods to Get More Customers. Recuperado 5 octubre, 2019, de https://www.crazycall.com/blog/sales-prospecting-methods

16. PADILLA, R. P. (n.d.). Prospection of Clients: Learn How to Do It Right. Retrieved October 5, 2019, from https://www.genwords.com/blog/prospeccion -de-clientes

17. Paul S. Goldner, P. S. G. (n.d.). Hot Prospecting - customer acquisition. Retrieved October 5, 2019, from

https://www.leadersummaries.com/resumen/prospeccion-en-caliente

18. Paula McKinney, P. M. (n.d.). Text Messaging Your Network Marketing Prospect. Retrieved October 5, 2019, from https://paula-mckinney.com/text-messaging-network-marketing-prospect/

19. Press office, P. O. (2019, 22 May). 6 tips to get the most out of your CRM - redk ES. Retrieved October 5, 2019, from https://www.redk.net/es-ES/blog/crm-6-consejos-aprovechar-maximo/

20. Sales prospection | Socialetic. (2013, 17 December). Retrieved October 5, 2019, from https://www.socialetic.com/prospeccion-de-ventas.html

21. What is CRM: Customer Relationship Management and CRM Software. (s.f.-a). Retrieved October 5, 2019, from https://www.sumacrm.com/soporte/que-es-crm

22. What is CRM: Customer Relationship Management and CRM Software. (s.f.-b). Retrieved October 5, 2019, from https://www.sumacrm.com/soporte/que-es-crm

23. What the client and your prospects want. (2012, 14 December). Retrieved October 5, 2019, from http://blog.brainstormer.es/que-quiere-el-cliente-y-tus-prospectos/

24. Sarah Kathleen Peck, S. K. P. (2018, 7 junio). The Art of Asking: Or, How to Ask And Get What You Want. Recuperado 5 octubre, 2019, de https://medium.com/startup-pregnant/the-art-of-asking-or-how-to-ask-and-get-what-you-want-9e7455ca375b

25. Shane Barker, S. B. (2019, 2 octubre). 7 Simple Ways to Drive Sales on Social Media (With Examples). Recuperado 5 octubre, 2019, de https://medium.com/better-marketing/7-simple-ways-to-drive-sales-on-social-media-with-examples-8012193aa2fb

26. SONIA DURIO LIMIA, S. D. L. (n.d.) What is Social Selling and how can it make you sell more? Retrieved October 5, 2019, from https://josefacchin.com/social-selling-que-es/

27. Tom Smith, T. O. M. (2014, 14 febrero). 8 Benefits of Customer Relationship Management Software. Recuperado 5 octubre, 2019, de http://www.insightsfromanalytics.com/blog/bi d/374342/8-benefits-of-customer-relationship-management-software

28. WENDY CONNICK, W. C. (2019, 31 julio). Meaning of WIIFM in Sales Keeping Prospect's Needs Top of Mind. Recuperado 5 octubre, 2019, de https://www.thebalancecareers.com/what-is-wiifm-2917381

29. How to assemble the best customer prospecting strategy? (2018, 7 December). Retrieved October 5, 2019, from

https://blog.hotmart.com/es/prospeccion-de-clientes/

30. What is segmentation in marketing? LCMK. (2019, 12 March). Retrieved October 5, 2019, from https://laculturadelmarketing.com/que-es-segmentar-en-marketing/

31. What is a CRM? Understands what a CRM is and what it offers to the different areas of a company. (n.d.). Retrieved October 5, 2019, from https://www.elegircrm.com/crm/que-es-un-crm